HalleluYah for Life : 93 to Infinity

Grass Hippies Productions | QaraYah Productions LLC.

Copyright © 2019 by Kha'irah Nairobi Cook

ISBN: 978-0-578-51500-7

It Was Until It Wasn't
(The Reason I Haven't Responded)
Book of Poems & Depictions

Written & Drawn By

Kha'irah Nairobi Cook

Here's to you . . .

It Was Until It Wasn't
(The Reason I Haven't Responded)
Book of Poems and Depictions

Introduction:

I wrote you a poem based on how we were getting
along, entitled, "we should've waited."
That was pretty much the beginning of the end
for the relationship, we were in.

This book includes poems from a relationship past.
Each poem was inspired by real-life situations. They are
in order by situation most have dates some don't.

Take a journey with me exploring the up and down
ride of this emotional rollercoaster.

The Reason

This Time Spent . . .

Somethings just shouldn't be. The
greatest mystery is to have a love
that truly cares for me.
Left with nothing but an empty space,
just to see you pass my way. I have
to say this is just a running joke
you'd hope doesn't replay.
I laughed at the thought of me
and you, now it must be true.
You can't hope to find love when
love has a different definition
to you.
Taking chances just to get rejected
it's become what we had expected,
a love lost just like they projected.

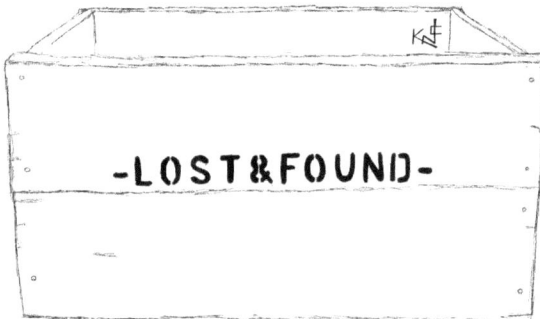

Untitled (Love Tornado)

Spent time just to feel
neglected.
It's so sad when you're
everything I expected.
I ask myself every day is
this what I really want?
You answered that question for me,
and it's nothing I would have guessed.
It's stupid to think this was
more than what it was before.
This time spent still leaves me
questioning, was it worth it?
I don't think so. I hope to wake up
tomorrow and possibly know
the meaning to this love tornado.

I've Lost It

Silly of me to think
this would work

Love is just a word

Energy is real

And I should have never
done this

He thinks it's time to
jump ship.

I've lost my love and best friend

And now all I can say
is okay . . .

I guess this is the end.

FIN.

Those Words

If you loved me, you would see those
words you chose will always make you lose.
Stupid is a word used lightly in spite of me.
I sit and listen to your stupidity and
it's mind blowing to me,
how you could think the shit you
say is true.
Only true for who? Me or you?
Who's wrong? Who's singing a sad song?
Barely speak, just so we can get along.
Whatever, I'm tired of this backwards ass
love song.

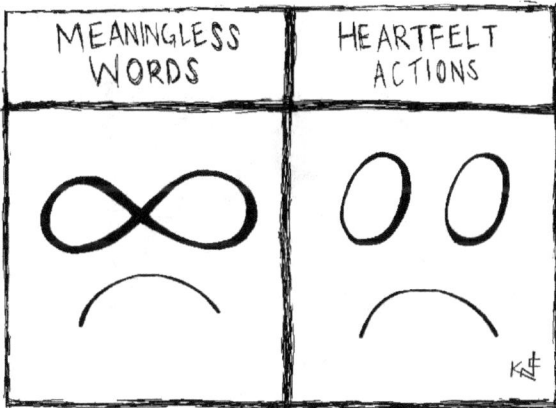

Limitations

Some allow others to set limits in
their lives, while you set limits
in your own life.

If you can't be you, who will?

If you're scared to live, why do it?

If you're worried about what someone
will think, stay home

If you limit yourself, are
you truly being yourself?

If I Cared

If I cared what people
thought of me I wouldn't
be me.

I would be a made up
character in someone's
head.

Never fully developed.

Still worried.

Missing out on life.

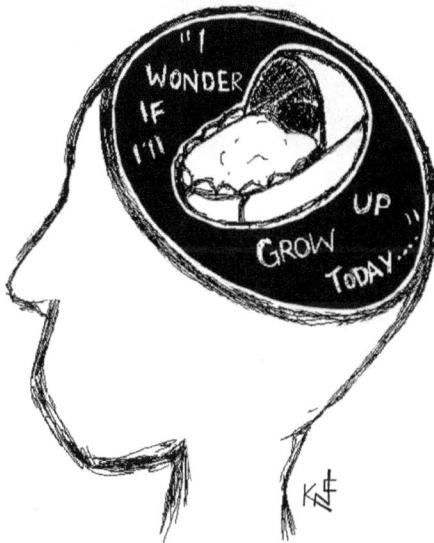

A Sad Day

You flipped
To take the blame off you
You flipped

So, What Now?

So, what now, what now . . .
you're not around.
Played yourself like a clown.
Dopest in town.
Boo'd up to who's up.
Still the shit.
You regret it.
"Get back with you", that
statement is past tense.
Lived it, loved it, had it,
had you,
now I'm onto something new,
who would've knew.

Forever Is Not Enough

Forever is not enough
for all of my love and trust
forever is not enough.

They say forever and a day
I say if you stay then
you stay.

Show me who you really
are.
A star? A dreamer who
wants to drive fast cars?

Nah, not that, I know who
you are, someone pretending
that they know what it
takes to be a star.

Never use words to show
you're hurt, it'll just make
it worse.
Do your words leave scars?

Because those words you used
seemed like a curse.

But tell the truth come
clean show me what you
really mean.

You'd said you'd stay
forever & a day, yet still
you went away.

So, all I have to say is
If you stay, then you stay.
And fuck forever that bitch
wasn't my friend anyway.

You Left

You left
You left to a world
where they put you in a box.

You left
You left to join the world
unfit for our kind.

You left
You left what seemed
to be the darkness for
the "light".

You left
You left not realizing you
need darkness to see
the light.

The dark & light are
one, the chosen are aware
and life's just begun.

You left
You left for lies instead of truth.

You left
You left you . . .

The real you . . .

You left
You left you . . .

And that's what you
chose to do.

So, the blame is on
you.

"WHERE DID
HE GO?"

"HE LEFT"

It Flows

I've cried a lot, you
told me it was okay
to cry until it turned
you into the bad guy.

Crying wasn't a trait
of mine. Then we spent
time. A lot of shit got
put on the line.

Time after time. Cry
after cry. I watched
this love roll by. Flying
high almost to kiss the sky.

So much time has
passed now, and I
want you to know I
no longer cry over
you in my room alone.

Wait

I waited for you
to see if this thing
was true.
I waited to see
what you would
do . . .

Wait broke
the wagon and the
shit was true.
What you did, you
shouldn't do . . . I
waited to see the
real you.

When

I loved you when
I wasn't supposed
to . . ..

Now I see why ...

Wrote some poems
today and the shit
made me cry.

Someone Who Knows

I need someone who knows
how dope I am without the
help of someone else.
I need someone who knows
the shit is real.
I need some who knows I
am not replaceable.
I need someone who knows ...

What Happened?

I wanted you, I had you,
you left me.
I waited for you,
you came back,
I loved you.
You left me, you thought
it was easy.
You came back,
But I'm not that easy.

Love?

When I love someone I
love them whole heartedly.
You made me feel stupid
for loving you.
Now what I am to do,
you're back like this
love was an easy renew.
Asking for a redo. Could
this be true or is this the
same shit we already
went through?

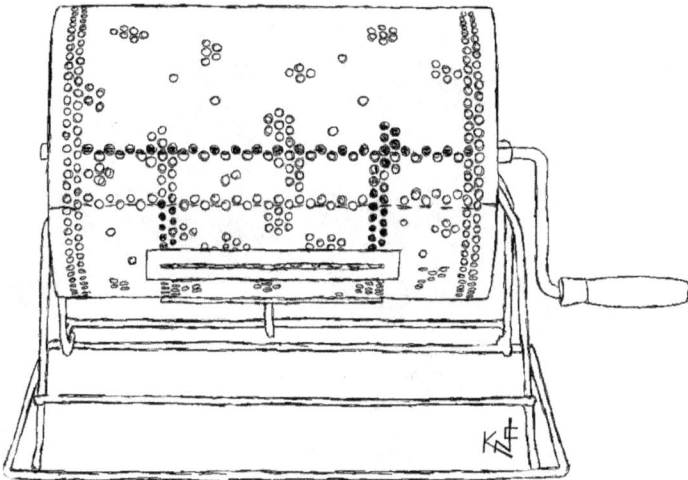

Emotions

Lately I've been writing
out my emotions hoping
that one day I'll show
them.

They are the feelings and
words that have been
left unspoken.

You were the one that
I had chosen.

Now my heart sometimes
feels frozen.

I wish I had said those
words unspoken.

WHAT?

. . . . . nothing

KN‡

The Shit You Say

My heart is tight and
my eyes keep shining
light.

I'm at a loss for words
and emotions.

So much has happened since the
last time we've spoken,
face to face in the same
space.

My heart is tight.

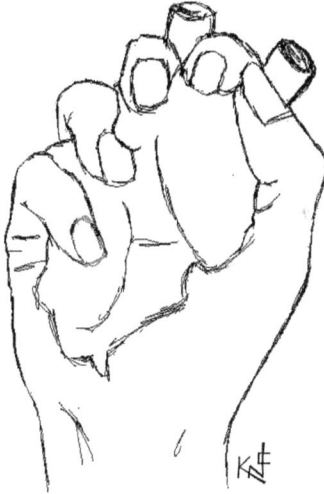

A Mistake?

You said it was a mistake
4 months and 1 day too late.

My heart aches because I
don't know what to say.

It's been 4 months and 1
day.

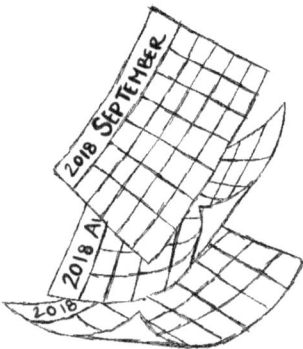

Choices Were Made

There was a day when you
choose someone or something
else over me and you left.
You really left.
You told me it would be
easier apart. You said you
enjoyed what we had, but
that still didn't help us last.
As of late I've been thinking
a lot of the past, and it makes
me sad. You were the one I
was so happy to have.
You choose someone or
something over me. How
could this be? I had chosen
you to live infinite with me.
You told me you didn't want
a relationship so quickly
you dipped. But now you've
slipped back to my front
door saying it's not easy
anymore.

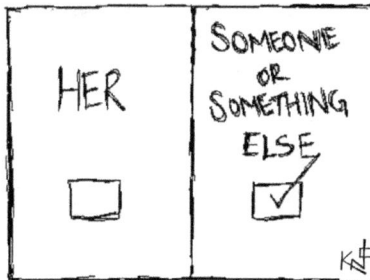

Your Love

The love that you're asking
for doesn't live here anymore.
It flew the coop just like you.
But the thing is there is no
return policy for the love you
seek. So, I guess you should've
kept the receipt.

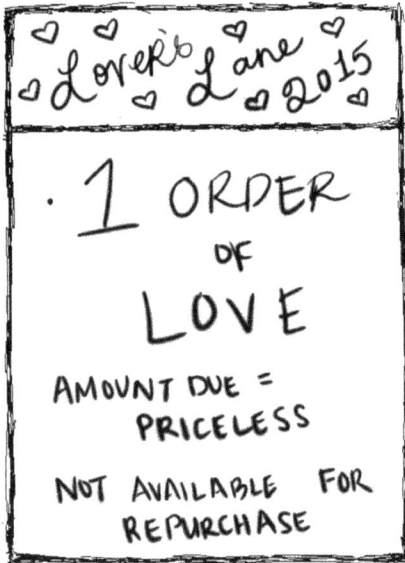

EMAL

So, it seems you can't
be cool without me, your
whole personality changed.
It's strange and such as
a shame you've become
such a lame.

i'm sorry....
do i know
you?   Kat

Some Days

Some days I think about
you and what we'd do.
At times, I still can't
believe it's true.

Thanks?

I'm connecting with new people
and I'm having new experiences
too. This would have never
happened but it's all because of
you. I guess you could say this
is a thank you?

Just for you

I hope you're okay,
I see you sometimes
just for a split second.
I hope you're okay, I
can see regrets on
your face.
I hope you're okay ...
That's all I really
have to say.

I care for
your
well-being....

KNF

Blocked

You blocked me so you
wouldn't have to look
at me.
What am I to say when
you still say "I love you"
anyway.

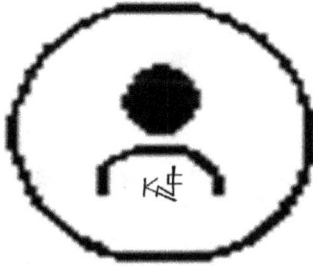

No Posts Yet

Programming

You offered your love after
you took your love away.
Not once but twice almost
in the exact same way.
The only difference was the
person telling you it'll be
okay.
On the flip side
How am I supposed to trust
anything you say?

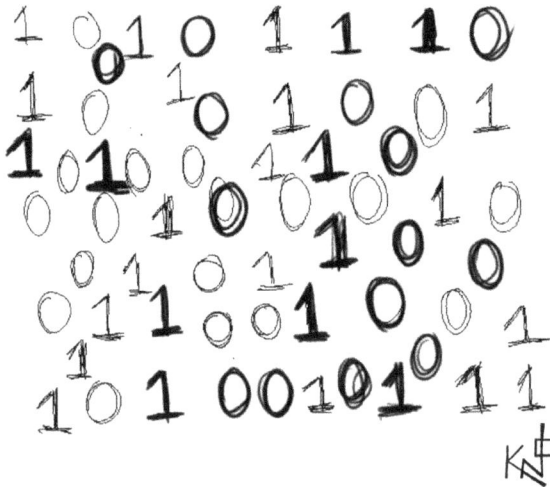

1 0 0 1 0 1 1 1 0
1 0 1 0 1 0 0 1
1 0 1 0 0 1 1 0 0 1
0 0 1 0 0 0 1 0 0
0 1 1 0 1 1 0 0
0 1 1 0 0 1 0 0 0 1
1 0 1 0 0 1 0 1 0 1 1

What You Were

You were more than
just a love. You were
family, not to just
me but to my actual
family.

This Life

Choices have been made.
Players have been played.
Slayers have been slayed.
And that bed has been
made.

You Are So Whack

So, it seems you have something
you want to show off.
This has to be some of the funniest
shit I've ever seen, that's not
even you that's making the scene.
I laugh at the fact that you
thought that would spark
something in me.

I DGAF ABOUT you & I DGAF ABOUT THAT!

I Liked You

Ridiculous to think I
actually, liked you.
Because like is different
than love, I liked you.
Well the you I thought
I knew. Seems to be I
liked someone that
wasn't you.

A Thought

It's crazy when you
almost begin to miss
someone and then they
show you why not to.

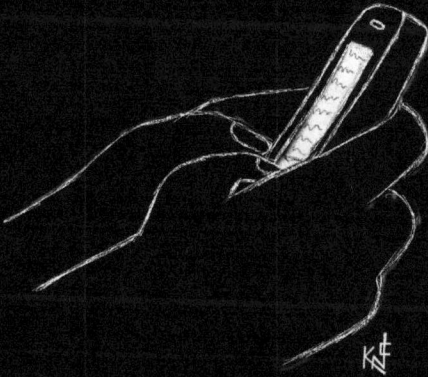

Silly

It's a shame I never
thought you'd be this
lame.

Confidence

This world needs someone
who has true confidence
in themselves.
Who knows they can do
it because they put their
mind to it. And someone
else's "you can do it" is
just a reassurance.

Be your own inspiration

"I
AM
SO
IMPRESSED
BY
YOU."

Started: 11.10.18
Completed: 1.23.19

What I Need

Show me that you're able to grow.
Show me that you know what it
takes to make my love flow,
If not, please let go.

Me

I am a once in a lifetime
type of person . . .

((. . . once
in a
Lifetime))

www.ingramcontent.com/pod-product-compliance
Lightning Source LLC
Chambersburg PA
CBHW071439040426

42445CB00012BA/1393